The Holistic Educators:

Education for the 21st century

by Cara Martin

The Educational Heretics Series

Published 1997 by Educational Heretics Press
113 Arundel Drive, Bramcote Hills, Nottingham NG9 3FQ

British Cataloguing in Publication Data.
A catalogue record for this book is available from the British Library

Martin, Cara
        The Holistic Educators:
        Education for the 21st century

ISBN   1-900219-08-5

Design and production: Educational Heretics Press

Printed by Esparto, Slack Lane, Derby DE22 3DS

For my daughter, Maddy,
who taught me more than I ever taught her.

Author's Note

Some of the personal reflections in this book reveal the author's essentially Christian perspective. A holistic approach to education does not, however, depend upon a a Christian view. Rather it rests upon a broad-based consensus amongst those from a variety of religious, non-religious and philosophical traditions, that the nature of reality is ultimately spiritual.

Precisely what this means to each individual is the essence of the spiritual quest as it becomes refined in experience and reflection. It is a quest upon which so many 'educational heretics' have embarked and which leads each individual along their own path to understanding. Along this personal educational journey, we are able to learn from each other through dialogue, interaction, and co-operation. It is a quest which those who would guide the learner along the way can aim to understand and support, but one for which there can be no substitute by even the most well-intentioned of educators.

Contents

This book is dedicated to the memory of
Ivy Meighan

Educational Heretics Press
exists to question
the dogmas of education in general,
and schooling in particular.

Introduction

I took my daughter out of school for the first time in the Spring of 1972. Maddy had enjoyed her early years at our local village school, but problems began when we moved house just before she was seven. Her new school looked idyllic. Housed in a thatched doll's house of a building overlooking the village green, it seemed perfect - but Maddy hated it.

A week or two after she first started at this new school we arrived one morning rather late, hastening into the building under the disapproving gaze of the Head Teacher watching from his office window. As we entered the cloakroom Maddy began to sob: *"Please Mummy don't make me go to school, please Mummy."*

Despite my personal doubts about the education system, at this point I was determined to try to be a "sensible" parent. I was therefore attempting to enforce the "common sense" view that this was just a temporary problem of adjustment to a new school; and that Maddy would soon settle down when she had made new friends and got used to her new teacher. I removed her coat, and hung it up, insisting that of course she had to go to school. Maddy clung screaming to a coat peg. Firmly, I pulled her from it and started to march her to the classroom door. But suddenly I had a flash-back to a memory of my own childhood: a vivid memory of my own mother dragging me screaming from a coat peg in another school cloakroom many years before. At five years old I had vowed that I would never do that to a child of mine.

By then at the classroom door, I turned around, grabbed Maddy's hand and announced, *"Come on, we're going home"*. We marched back out of the building again - this time beneath the somewhat startled gaze of the Headmaster. I wish I could say she never went back. But the following autumn we moved house yet again - this time to a nearby city. Here I came under considerable pressure from the welfare officer attached to the local school to return Maddy to formal education. So she went back to an infant and junior school which had a reputation as being one of the best in the city. By the following spring a child who had loved books since babyhood would no longer allow me even to read her a bedtime story - such was her fear of not being able to meet the demands of her teachers that it was now high time she should be able to read.

One night when Maddy again turned away from a once-favourite book that I had offered to read her at bed time, I recognized that if this continued my child really **would** end up illiterate - through fear. For her "education" was building within her a fear block of the written word, from which, I felt, she might never recover.

We gave up our little terraced house in the city, and escaped the well-meant attentions of the education welfare officer by spending the summer in a caravan in the garden of a friend's family home. And Maddy finally left school behind her once and for all.

That summer she learnt to swim. I had decided to leave anything directly associated with school and her formal education completely to one side for the summer, and just let her explore and play in the meadows and woods with which we were surrounded. The grounds of our friend's house sloped down to a magical lake, and in the shallow waters at the lake's edge Maddy taught herself to swim. I can vividly recall the look of joy on her face, and her sense of triumph, as she demonstrated her achievement to me for the first time. She had learnt to do something all by herself, and now she knew she could do it again. Two weeks later she learnt to read.

As the autumn approached once more, I had bought her a couple of little first readers. One of these was in rhyme, something Maddy had loved and responded to since she was very tiny. We read through this little book together several times and within a week she knew it off by heart and could read it by herself. Within two, she had discovered that she could also read the other book I had bought her. All the agony and the angst about her not being able to read had been overcome in a matter of two weeks, with two books - and **no pressure**.

I had learnt the first rule of a new approach to education: that children naturally want to learn - all they need is encouragement and a little adult support and they will learn in their own way with an ease and fluency that makes the best endeavours of our formal education system appear stilted, clumsy and unnecessary. What Maddy taught me at that time was to become the basis of my educational work for the next twenty years. This book is the product of those years of educating my own daughter, and later a group of other children, outside the formal education system.

Chapter one

A personal experience

A new beginning

In the heady days of the early nineteen-seventies, it seemed possible that humanity was about to achieve everything we had ever dreamed of. So when I took Maddy out of school I had great hopes that we would soon discover some imaginative and exciting new option for her education. Our trial and error efforts to find this took us the length and breadth of Britain, but again and again we were disappointed.

Finally, Maddy started to attend a new "Free School" which was being set up by a group of parents and teachers in the area where we were living. She was happy there, but for a number of reasons the experiment only survived for two years. This was primarily because the premises which the school had used free of charge were sold when the generous owners moved house. However many of the parents and other adults who had run the school on the basis of their voluntary labour, also found it increasingly difficult to continue to give so much of their time and energy without payment.

The educational co-operative of parents and teachers, which was the option upon which we finally embarked, evolved slowly. In our dealings with the education authority the Free School group had decided not to register itself as a "school", as this would immediately have made us subject to all kinds of rules and regulations, such as minimum window area in relation to square footage of classroom. We therefore chose instead to become an educational "co-operative", with each parent taking their own child out of school, and taking legal responsibility for their education themselves in accordance with the provisions of the 1944 Education Act, (now replaced by the provisions of the 1993 Education Act).

Two children - my own daughter and another slightly older girl - remained out of school when the Free School closed down, and our "Co-operative" started with just these two children. Slowly we were joined by other local children who were either themselves desperately unhappy in school, or whose parents were dissatisfied with the education they were receiving in mainstream schools.

Organisation

Our early efforts were very disorganised and chaotic, and it was the children themselves who insisted we create more structure and organisation in their education. One of my most important educational lessons came from this experience, for whilst we adults were assuring our children that any structure to their education was completely unnecessary, and that they could be "learning all the time", (Holt, 1991), our children were demanding "timetables"; "school holidays" and "proper" work!

The great Italian educator Maria Montessori, (1984), suggests that children have a very deep-seated need for order, both in their environment and in their daily lives; and many people who are familiar with young children know how much they dislike disturbance to their regular routine.

What we had to learn in those heady days when true human freedom first appeared to be a realisable possibility, was that whilst human beings have freedom of spirit and freedom of mind, our Earthly environment is a structured world of forms. Part of humanity's "learning experience" here on Earth is therefore to recognise and accept the necessity for these structural limits, before we can reach a point of consciousness where we are able to transcend them.

So it appears that many children actually need a clearly organised structure to their educational work, and greatly enjoy the sense of orderly security with which it provides them. Nevertheless, like adults, children are all very different in their approach to life and learning, and perhaps the best we can hope to achieve is some reasonable balance between the creative freedom of the spirit-mind, and the limitations and demands of earthly structure.

In attempting to find this sort of balance between freedom and organisation, Maria Montessori suggested an important educational concept. She proposed that children should be given freedom to learn in their own way and their own time, within an environment which had been carefully structured and prepared to maximise their learning potential. Whilst in practice, Montessori developed her concept of the educational environment only in respect of her range of educational equipment and the classrooms that accommodated it. In Section III of this book a much broader understanding of the "educational environment" will be considered in the form of an educational community.

The Educational Co-operative

Once we had come through the initial confusion of our early struggles to establish our educational co-operative, we gradually organised ourselves so that the children spent one "session", (either a morning or an afternoon), with each adult involved in the group. At first most of these adults were parents, but in the later stages of the group's life we found a number of other adults who were also interested in becoming involved.

So a pattern emerged in which the children went to one of the adults in the group on Monday morning to do needlework or cookery; and to another on Monday afternoon to do art. On Tuesday they were with yet another adult all day doing English in the morning, and environmental studies and gardening in the afternoon. Wednesday was a day for individually chosen activities. My own daughter chose to do English Literature and History with her father on that day, whilst others did gymnastics at the local gym or went to other specialist subject groups of their own choice. On Thursday a friend came to do "maths" and "science" with the children, and on Friday morning another did Biology. Friday afternoon was again a time of "free choice", but also time to complete the record of the weeks activities which was contained in the children's "Portfolios" of work. These Portfolios were simple A4 folders into which the children placed a selection of their formal written work, together with examples of their art work, poetry, stories and other items of interest such as theatre programmes, magazine or newspaper cuttings, personal photographs, etc. The children were in full control of what they did, or did not, include in these Portfolios, and they quickly built up into attractive records of their various activities. The only "compulsory" element in keeping their Portfolios was that each week the children were expected to write up a brief record of that week's activities for the benefit of the education inspectors, and for this purpose their Portfolios proved an invaluable record.

The outcome

Our method of organising the children's work now seems to me to be far too "subject based", and if we were doing it again I would structure their education much more clearly around their own interests and enthusiasms. Nevertheless, in practice the mix was very flexible, and there were many days when they spent long hours learning musical instruments, writing plays and songs, or performing their musical productions before an appreciative audience of family and friends. They spent the whole of one summer creating a circus performance under the supervision of two friends with some basic skills in that area. On sunny days "mathematics" might be abandoned in favour of a walk to the local river where the children could swim in the mill pool, or they could visit the bluebell wood in spring. Some days we went swimming at the local pool, on others we went to the beach

At the beginning and end of each term we had a co-op meeting in which both children and adults had a vote, and where the programme for the following months was discussed with each child and their parents. As far as possible we tried to accommodate the children's own interests, and to find teachers in areas where they expressed a wish to learn. Most of the time we succeeded, although it sometimes proved impossible. We never did find Maddy an Italian teacher; nor did the eldest boy in the group ever find someone with whom to explore the relationship between nuclear physics and world religions! (Unfortunately, this was before Capra, (1983), had written his marvellous book, *The Tao of Physics,* in which he explores the parallels between modern physics and Eastern mystical religions).

Looking back, many of the mistakes we made are all too obvious, and if we were starting again we could, of course, do much better. But for the most part the children were occupied and happy, and they have all ended up as interesting and capable human beings. As adults, all of these young people are literate and competent; but far more important, all are also self-directed and creative.

Quite of her own accord, Maddy chose to take "O" Levels. Having successfully completed these from home, she went on to our local College of Further Education to do "A" level Drama and English, and from there to drama school in London. For many years a member of an all-girl singing group, Maddy has now chosen to make her career in the music business, and is the Studio Manager of one of London's largest recording studios. Two other former members of the group worked for the BBC before leaving to start their own families, and one is an acrobat, who has travelled the world with a well-known company. Another former student trained to be a dancer, and yet another is a musician.

Chapter two

Holistic education today

The wood or the trees?

When Maddy was about six years old she came home from school one afternoon to join me in the community cafe where I was working as a volunteer. Sitting down at one of the tables, she announced that she had made up a poem and asked me to write it down for her. It went like this:

> *I look at the tree*
> *And what do I see?*
> *The beautiful flower*
> *And a big velvet bee.*

I do not know enough about poetic metre and rhyming structure to be sure whether this technically fits the formal structure of Japanese Haiku poetry, but it seems to me to be true to the Zen spirit and simplicity of such poems. Yet when Maddy dictated this poem to me she was still at the school, which almost put her off literacy for life. In their narrowly defined concern with the mechanics of literacy, her teachers had quite failed to recognise or encourage the genuine interest in the flow and feel of language which Maddy so clearly revealed in this little poem.

When our children are learning to walk or talk we do not doubt that they will master these extraordinarily complex skills. We simply assume their capability, and encourage the child's natural process. Some are quicker than others, and that is considered perfectly normal. For we recognise that average ages of achievement are precisely that - **average**. Statistically, an average can only have meaning if it embraces a span - so some children learn to walk when they are nine months and some do not master the skill until they are eighteen months or even older. If we categorised the eighteen month old walkers as 'failures', referring them to specialists, psychologists and therapists, and generally communicating to them our own extreme anxiety about their 'failure', we might suddenly find that we had achieved the extraordinary feat of creating children who really could not learn to walk - because they were so terrified of failing!

Yet this is what we do to many of our children in schools. We fuss and fume about their ability to achieve narrowly defined attainment targets by a particular age, and end up unable to recognise the wider meaning and purpose of their education because of our over-concern with particular narrow objectives. A classic case of being unable to see the wood for the trees!

What do we want for our children?

In considering children's educational needs it is important first to consider why we want them to be educated at all. For the effectiveness of particular educational methods can only be assessed in the light of the purposes they are intended to serve.

So what do we mean by a 'good education'? What is the point of it all? Should our education system be designed primarily to ensure that all children obtain high level academic qualifications and thus secure a passport to well-paid employment? Do we expect all children to become highly paid professionals, or intellectual experts? Would there be enough jobs for them all, even if they were all able to do so? Or are we more concerned to ensure that our children are aware enough of the choices that are open to them in a modern western society to be capable of choosing for themselves a way of life with which they are at peace?

The traditional approach to education through formal schooling that has developed in western societies has often been justified on the grounds that it is necessary to initiate children into a common cultural heritage. It is suggested that only through familiarity with what society as a whole has identified as the best and most worthwhile aspects of our cultural tradition - those aspects that have been organised and systematised into clearly defined forms of knowledge, ('subjects' to most of us!), - can children be considered 'educated'. In recent years, however, the educational debate has been focused not so much on the value of young people understanding our cultural tradition as on the importance of an educated workforce to the economic future of our society.

Whilst it is clear that a state-funded education system will inevitably need to consider whether, as a society, we are getting 'value for money' from the increasingly expensive education provided for our young citizens, nevertheless, as was pointed out in a recent letter to the press:

> "Children do not exist to fuel economic growth ... They exist in their own right as persons. Of course learning to be competent and to contribute to the community's well-being is a vital element in the growth of a person, but it is only one side of the story. Education conceived entirely in instrumental terms, whether for the honing of a fine tool in the economy, or for furthering personal ambition to "get on", is out of balance.
>
> The young have other needs as well: to explore a fascinating world beyond themselves; to develop a critical mind; to discover who they are through constructive and stable relationships; to form long-term purposes and practise the discipline needed to pursue them."

Marjorie Reeves, St Anne's College, Oxford. Letter to *The Independent* 18 February, 1997.

We cannot confine our conception of education to the development of a well educated labour force to service the country's economy. For children are parts of a far greater whole than the particular nation into which they are born, and their education needs to be designed to develop them not simply as efficient workers, but as effective human beings.

Education and the holistic world view

From a holistic perspective it is recognised that in our complex modern society it is clearly useful for children to have an ability to read and write with ease, and a grasp of mathematics that at least enables them to check their supermarket bill. Nevertheless, "education" is understood as something much broader than such basic skills, broader even than high levels of academic success. This wider view of the purpose of education is indeed supported by many educational professionals, but what most clearly distinguishes a holistic approach to education is the underlying world view upon which it is based.

In recent years, humanity's conception of the nature of physical reality has undergone such a dramatic transformation that it has been described as a paradigm shift. Classical physics was based on the 'common sense' assumption that we live in a world of separate physical forms each of which is made up of smaller particles, whether cells, molecules or atoms. Modern physics, however, is beginning to reveal that the ultimate nature of these apparently solid material forms has nothing to do with any physical substance, but is, in fact, a form of energy.

Science today is coming to recognise that we live in a universe made up entirely of energy - an interactive web of energy that is interconnected and interdependent, in which nothing can be understood as an isolated entity, but only as parts of an integrated whole. Whilst aspects of this interactive energy system appear to our senses as separated and isolated, in reality these apparently separate forms are merely temporary patterns in a universal energy flow - whirlpools in the universal energy ocean. This new holistic world view acknowledges that ultimately all life's apparently separate forms are, in fact, united in a single 'whole'. Whether stars or rocks, plants, animals, or human beings, it is coming to be understood that all such apparently separate forms are, in reality, parts of a single unified energy system.

Increasingly we are also coming to understand the truth that spiritual teachers down the ages have tried to explain: that uniting these apparently separate elements is a powerful force of attraction which, in the physical world, is described as the force of gravity, but which human beings experience as love.

Whilst older generations still struggle to understand the nature of the changes that have taken place in humanity's understanding of the world, this new perspective has been quickly appreciated by the open minds of the young. *"One Life", "One World", "One Love"*; sang the heroes of the youth revolution; and the young heard their call, and responded with joy. This changed understanding of the nature of reality has yet to be reflected in our political and social organisation, however, for many of those with political and social power have so far failed to understand the implications of this new world view.

Out of our growing understanding of the world view being revealed by modern science, a new conception of the meaning and purpose of education is beginning to be developed - an understanding that can perhaps best be described as 'holistic education'. For education is increasingly understood as a subtle evolutionary process, through which each individual comes to understand themselves more fully, and is enabled to explore and express their relationship to that greater 'whole' that is all Life.

A model of holistic education

From this holistic perspective, it is recognised that human consciousness embraces many different levels. The three primary levels of human awareness being the physical, emotional, and mental, each of which is enfolded within the ultimate spiritual consciousness of which we are all a part.

This conception of education can be represented diagrammatically as in Figure 1. (overleaf). Arising from the source, represented in the diagram as Point A, the three interlocking inner circles represent the three levels of human consciousness. These are enfolded within the universal 'whole' that is 'All Life', and which is represented in the diagram by Circle B. Our relationship to the 'whole' is now understood as our primary relationship. It is that spiritual relationship between humanity and 'all Life' that mystics of many cultures have struggled down the years to explain to an uncomprehending world.

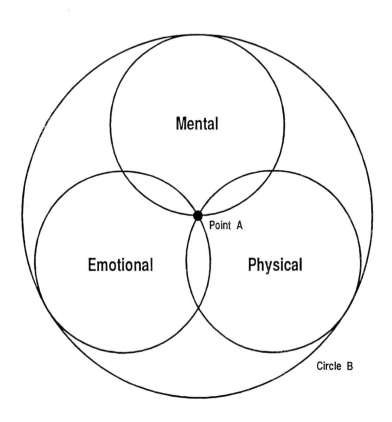

Figure 1

The basic model of holistic education represented in Figure 1. aims to explain the relationship between this educational approach and the underlying world view upon which it is based. It is intended to provide a framework from which to understand the overall approach to education offered by a holistic perspective.

Criteria of an holistic approach to education

A more detailed model of holistic education is illustrated in Figure 2. (overleaf). This delineates a series of more fully defined criteria which aim to distinguish some of the most essential elements of this educational approach.

In this section these criteria will be examined more fully, and an attempt will be made to demonstrate how each is essential to a holistic - or 'whole person' - approach to education.

1. Holistic

A central premise of a holistic approach to education is that, by its very nature, education is holistic, for it involves the often subtle interaction of all levels of human being in the context of that greater spiritual 'whole' that is All Life. In attempting to define the purpose of holistic education, the first criteria I have developed therefore states that:

> *The purpose of holistic education is to develop all levels of human being - physical, emotional and mental - and to integrate them in the context of the spiritual whole that is all Life.*

i. The pieces of the jig-saw

At the age of sixteen when I first began to discover the real joy of intellectual understanding, I framed a modest ambition - I decided that I wanted to learn everything there was to know about everything in the world! My efforts got me as far as developing an interest in the French Impressionist painters before my enthusiasm for the task began to wane.

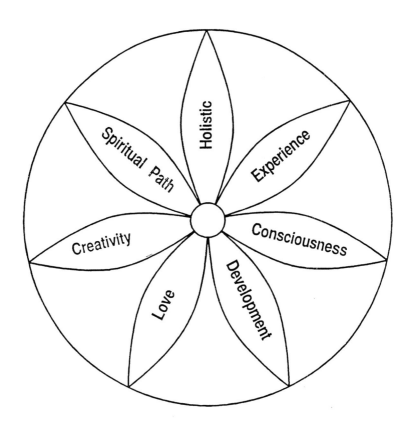

Figure 2

Looking back, I can see that what I was actually seeking was not detailed knowledge of everything there is to know, which even then I really knew to be impossible, but some sort of integrating framework for all those infuriating snippets of knowledge that I had gleaned from my years of formal schooling: factual information about Romans and Tudors, photosynthesis, Pythagorean theorems, Shakespeare and the Romantic poets. What did it all add up to? What did it all mean?

I can still recall my delight when, at the age of eighteen, in my first year of University, I discovered that history and geography were related! For it is the unrelatedness, the disconnectedness, of much of our learning in school that proves so frustrating and confusing to children trying to make sense of their world. In a famous critique of the American school system entitled, *Dumbing us Down,* John Taylor Gatto (1992) explains the problem when he suggests that: *"Meaning, not disconnected facts, is what sane human beings seek, and education is a set of codes for processing raw data into meaning."* And yet this award-winning American teacher is driven to acknowledge that conventional schooling too often teaches only, *"the un-relating of everything ... disconnections ... an infinite fragmentation the opposite of cohesion."*

From a holistic perspective, therefore, an essential quality of this educational approach is to assist young learners in the process of integrating their learning into a coherent and meaningful 'whole', for it is recognised that the relevance and value of individual events, theories and facts are revealed only in their relationship to a wider context.

ii. Learning for living

The approach to learning embraced in holistic education is not just about finding an integrated intellectual framework for **theoretical** learning, however. It is also about integrating learning and living. So whilst someone might choose to specialise in making furniture to earn a living, this work would be clearly understood as but one aspect of that person's whole-life picture - one aspect of their learning and development as creative human beings. For the aim of education is to enable students to develop and integrate into a balanced composition all aspects of their life and work, and to learn from all the experiences of their life in every field.

From a holistic perspective, therefore, education is not seen as being confined to purely theoretical or academic learning but includes the development of all aspects of human experience. For it is understood to be about developing and learning through all the levels of human being - physical, emotional, mental and spiritual - and integrating these into the learner's understanding of the world. This approach clearly distinguishes holistic education from the mainstream, where it is widely accepted that formal education should be confined to an understanding of, 'the things of the mind'. (Barrow and Woods, 1988).

This traditional approach to education which sees it as confined to academic understanding of particular subject areas, has been reaffirmed in Britain with the introduction of the National Curriculum, and meeting its tightly circumscribed demands now leaves teachers and schools with little time or energy for more integrated and holistic approaches to education.   Meantime, government quangos press energetically for the reinstatement of more formal teaching methods, and work hard on the vilification of 'progressive' methods which, it is claimed, have failed a whole generation of children. The simplistic terms in which the debate has been framed have been eagerly picked up by the media.

What is so extraordinary about the current debate, however, is that while politicians and the media use the needs of the economy to justify their demands that 'progressive' approaches to education be abandoned in favour of 'traditional' methods which concern themselves only with formal coverage of those 'subjects' that were considered essential to the 'educated man' in the early years of this century, employers themselves are starting to recognise the importance of a more holistic approach. For in recent months employers' organisations have publicly demanded a curriculum which embraces self-directed learning, team work, and personal growth.

The development of modern management techniques has involved a realisation of the value of what is often termed 'systems thinking'. This is understood as the ability to achieve a comprehensive overview of a situation, and to recognise the relationship of each of the parts in a particular situation or process to a greater whole - whether the whole in question is the organisational framework of a business, the international economy, or the evolving culture and value system of a nation. This ability, it has been realised, is what distinguishes truly creative managers and leaders from the mainstream.

Yet whilst employers plead for a wider vision of the meaning and purpose of education, politicians insist on a return to more traditional methods which encourage students to regurgitate their received knowledge through a process originally designed to keep Victorian children off the streets whilst their parents worked in the factories. It is a process that does not encourage children to think for themselves - let alone to think laterally or originally. But as employers are finding out to their cost, in an information-rich economy, those businesses that survive and grow are those whose workforce can comprehend complex data speedily and relevantly; who can interpret old information in new ways, and who can innovate and think creatively.   Prizes in a global economy do not go to those who are only capable of repeating the lessons of yesterday.   Sadly, it seems to be a lesson that politicians of all persuasions have yet to learn.

2. Experience

The second criteria that I have formulated to define a holistic approach to education proposes that:

> **Successful education is based on respect for the intrinsic worth of each individual learner, and an understanding of the validity and relevance of their own life experience.**

i. Learning all the time

From a holistic perspective it is understood that children's education is not confined to what they learn through formal instruction in schools, but embraces a far wider range of experience. For everything around them is education to a child, and they learn as much from a weekend in the country, or from listening to the social interaction between their mother and the next door neighbour as they do from a carefully prepared science lesson, or a discussion in Personal and Social Education. Children, and indeed adults, are learning all the time. Every life experience is also a learning experience, and it is impossible to separate the meaningful continuum of real life experience from the formal theoretical education received in schools, for one will inevitably influence and inform the other.

Whilst politicians of all persuasions pontificate about the importance of improving 'educational standards', and both teachers and parents now get the blame for children's failure to reach national norms in the three Rs, little mention is made of the importance of the child's home environment, or of its influence upon their formal education. Nevertheless, even a cursory glance at the league tables of attainment now published for all schools in Britain, quickly reveals what most educators have known for years: in terms of educational achievement - poverty shows. For poverty in financial terms almost inevitably translates into poverty of life experience. Children of wealthy parents tend to travel more frequently, and have a wide variety of books, videos, and CD-Roms at their disposal. They have their leisure, sporting and artistic interests supported financially, and meet more people socially. They have rooms of their own for quiet concentration, and gardens in which to play with their friends. Many of these opportunities to enrich their life experience are denied children from poor backgrounds, and their understanding of the world is restricted as a result.

"Ah!" say the politicians, *"but a difficult social background cannot be used as an excuse for poor educational standards."* In support of their argument they cite the wonderful achievements of some successful inner city schools working in socially deprived areas. And, as a teacher, it is of course important to encourage children from all social situations to believe in themselves and their chances of success. But that is not the same thing as saying that poverty and social disadvantage make no difference to a child's educational chances, because a substantial body of well-

documented research clearly demonstrates that they make an enormous difference. With a lot of goodwill, good resources and well organised work, social disadvantage can perhaps be alleviated, but poverty and experiential deprivation are still **disadvantages**.

If I were a teacher of physically disabled children I would, of course, encourage them to have faith in their own abilities, take on challenges, and believe that they were capable of creating worthwhile lives for themselves. But I could hardly be so cruel and insensitive as to pretend that physical disability is not a disadvantage in life. Yet this is precisely what politicians are doing with regard to social disadvantage.

ii. Experience and individual needs

From a holistic perspective it is understood that successful education needs to be based on the learner's individual level of experience, and that children who are deprived of a variety of interesting and stimulating experiences in their lives will be at a considerable disadvantage in the formal education system.

In some observations I made on a Montessori school in central London, I saw a clear example of this principle in practice. In the notes I made on that visit I wrote:

*"I recall my observations on the Green House Montessori School, and watching little Alice "take over" a wooden puzzle being tackled by another, less able, child. The "puzzle" was a very complex map of Europe, with each country a separate section. The child who had originally selected this ... hadn't a first clue about the meaning of this "map", and every move was entirely random. Four year old Alice arrived on the scene, however, and instantly knew **exactly** what she was doing - because she spent all her summer holidays touring Europe with her family, and had driven through most of the countries shown on the map..."*

Unfortunately our present approach to education quite fails to acknowledge that meaningful learning can only be based on the level of experience and understanding attained by each individual child. During another observation day I spent at an inner London comprehensive school I saw the sad educational results of this failure to acknowledge the vital importance of the child's level of individual experience.

I was sitting at the back of the classroom, observing a history lesson for 13 year olds which the very able young teacher was conducting in accordance with National Curriculum guidelines, when a young lad in front of me requested my help. The class was involved in answering a series of questions on a passage explaining the political intrigue surrounding the origins of the First World War, and both the language in which the passage was phrased, and its content, were highly complex. When I went over to help the boy it quickly emerged that he had been unable to take even the apparently obvious first step of reading the passage through. This was not because he could not read - but because he could not read language of that complexity well enough to make any sense at all of the passage in front of him. Despite his genuinely enthusiastic efforts to master the task, the whole exercise was therefore quite beyond his level of skill, and thus completely irrelevant to his individual educational needs.

How many times each day this ridiculous scenario is replayed in our schools hardly bears thinking about - nor does the waste of educational opportunities for the children, or the financial cost to the taxpayer. And all because, in designing our education system, we refuse to acknowledge the completely obvious fact that education can only be effective if it is based upon the level of experience and understanding attained by each individual child.

iii. The educational environment

Children's educational experience is also inevitably influenced by the physical environment in which they grow up. The importance of the educational effects of the child's environment is still largely unacknowledged in mainstream education, despite the growing evidence of its relevance to both children's social and intellectual development. Holistic education, however, recognises that the environment in which the child is educated will have a considerable influence on their development, for as Maria Montessori points out:

> *"The child has a different relation to his environment from ours. Adults admire their environment; they can remember it and think about it; but the child absorbs it. The things he sees are not just remembered; they form part of his soul. He incarnates in himself all in the world about him that his eyes see and his ears hear. In us the same things produce no changes, but the child is transformed by them."*

Maria Montessori, 1984, *The Absorbent Mind,* P. 69.

The environment in which they grow up makes a lasting impact on the sensitive minds of young children, and in many state schools today children quickly learn the social value and worth attributed to them by their society, simply by the state of their school buildings. Decaying buildings, broken equipment, peeling paint, and bleak asphalt playgrounds are often justified on the grounds that society can afford nothing better, but to the sensitive minds of young children they make a statement about how they are valued. It is hardly an accident that our most expensive private schools are located in gracious old buildings set in beautiful grounds. For this, too, is a message to the children who attend them: you are a valued human being and deserve a beautiful environment in which to spend your formative years. Messages about their social value start young for our children and are conveyed as much through their physical environment as through other, more obvious, social channels.

Many teachers are consciously or unconsciously aware of the significance of the environment to children, and make heroic efforts to create attractive surroundings for those in their care even within the rotting fabric of ageing school buildings. They give up hours of their free time to create beautiful displays of the children's art work. They spend their own money buying 'extras' to brighten drab classrooms, and create homely touches in quiet corners with carpets, cushions and plants. All this is recognised 'good practice' in many state schools, especially in primary schools. Whilst the psychological importance of a beautiful environment for older children is less acknowledged, nevertheless many educators recognise that shabby surroundings and decrepit equipment have an influence on children's attitude to their school and their work. If, as a society, we care so little about our children that we refuse to provide them with a decent environment in which to grow up, we can hardly be surprised when they respond by vandalising their dismal surroundings. Nor do we have to look far to see why so many react to our well-intentioned educational efforts with apathy and indifference, for in the very fabric of their physical surroundings we have unwittingly conveyed to them the message that indifference is the underlying truth of our attitude to them.

iv. The natural world

Many educators who adopt a 'whole person' approach to education also recognise the importance of the child's contact with the natural world. But again, the importance of this is not widely understood in mainstream education. Whilst nature walks were fashionable when I was a child, and environment education is increasingly accepted even in primary schools today, the real value of the child's contact with nature is still little appreciated.

Humanity has always drawn inspiration from the natural world. Theoretical scientists have learned from their observations of nature. Engineers have modelled man-made structures on natural designs. Artists have been inspired by it, and mystics on all spiritual paths have retreated to the wilderness to commune with the elements and draw inspiration from nature's harmonies.

For the natural world speaks to us of our interelatedness, and of the unity of the apparently separate elements in our earthly environment. It reminds us of the one-ness of all life. Whereas the man-made world speaks only of confusion, triviality, and separation. An afternoon in a busy shopping centre will all too often produce only exhaustion and irritability, whereas an afternoon walking by a tree-fringed lake calms, for it speaks of harmony and peace.

Holistic education recognises that children need to spend long hours in close contact with nature in all her moods. How many children will play happily in a puddle in the pouring rain - yet how few parents or teachers will allow them to do so? Is the condition of their fashionable clothing more important than the learning they achieve? Learning about the properties of water and the relationship of their bodies to this vital element is at stake. Perhaps, then, it is time to dispense with designer garments for toddlers and invest in some good wellington boots and other utilitarian clothing that does not hamper their development. Perhaps, too, it is time for children of all ages to be released from the enclosing walls of the classroom and returned to the arena in which children have always preferred to learn - the challenges and fascinations of the world of nature.

Holistic education is about making sense of our real life experience in real life settings - especially those provided by our most permanent and successful 'teacher' - our Mother Earth. For whilst the intellectual 'bodies of knowledge' that make up the material of the subject-based academic approach to education can sometimes assist us in making sense of our real life experience, they can never provide a substitute for it.

3. Consciousness

From a holistic perspective, education is understood as essentially a process of transforming consciousness. The third criteria of education therefore states that:

> *Education is a process of expanding individual consciousness to that of the greater whole of which we are all a part.*

i. The power of the mind

The power of the human mind in shaping our lives is only just beginning to be understood in western society, but a famous experiment in America illustrates this power particularly vividly. In her efforts to get her class to appreciate the effects of racial prejudice, a school teacher divided the class into two groups. The first group were those children in the class with blue eyes, and in the second were those who had brown eyes. For two weeks she consistently treated the blue-eyed group of children better than she treated those with brown eyes: they received more praise and encouragement, and were treated with respect and concern, whilst the brown-eyed children were treated with coldness and indifference. By the end of just two weeks the blue-eyed group of children were performing markedly above the rate of those children in the brown-eyed group. After two weeks she reversed the process, and treated the children with brown eyes better than those with blue. After a further two weeks the previous results were completely reversed, and it was now the group of brown-eyed children who were performing above the level of the others.

ii. The human mind

The human mind is often likened to a computer. The physical brain is seen as the computer hardware, and our personal consciousness as the programme. There is, however, a further dimension to the human mind, for human beings have a quality to their minds that enables them to make choices and take personal responsibility for them. To this extent we are unlike animals in that we can, to a high degree, choose, or modify, our own 'programmes'. It is that aspect of ourselves that we acknowledge when we say that we have free will. In the analogy with computers, this aspect of ourselves can perhaps only be understood in terms of the human designer of the computer programme, for no machine is yet able to choose its own destiny.

In so far as we have the freedom to choose our own mental 'programmes', human beings also have a very special responsibility. This responsibility is perhaps more obvious in the field of education than in any other human activity, for it is through education, and particularly through the education of our children, that our minds are most effectively 'programmed'. And as many of us have found to our cost, re-programming our mental computers later in life can be both difficult and time consuming.

Our ability to re-programme our mental 'computers' depends to a considerable extent upon our ability to critically re-examine our own thinking processes. Research evidence is now accumulating which demonstrates the importance to educational achievement of being taught basic thinking skills, but tuition in such skills is still very rare in our formal education. Nevertheless, in an article in The Times Educational Supplement, (TES 27 October 1995), Michael Barber drew attention to the results of an important research project entitled the CASE study which was conducted by King's College in London. This study found that:

> *"where secondary school pupils were taught not only science but how to think about science (and indeed how to think about how they were thinking) they did dramatically better in Science GCSE. Not only that, they did better in the other core subjects, too."*

In the same article Barber emphasised that there is now a substantial body of research evidence from all over the world that supports these same conclusions. Despite this evidence, however, governments continue to ignore the importance of including thinking skills in the curriculum of state schools, for as Barber points out: *"We are so obsessed with getting knowledge across that we miss the importance of the ability to use it."* Perhaps, however, there is a different reason why governments continue to ignore the importance of the evidence that clearly demonstrates that learning basic thinking skills can greatly improve educational standards, for as Hitler apparently once remarked: *"What good fortune for those in power that people do not think."*

iii. Consciousness and education

It is widely acknowledged that education has enormous power to transform our minds, particularly the minds of young children. However its very power in this respect is giving rise to increasing concern as education in Britain today becomes ever increasingly politicised. For education has, in fact, often been defined as a process of developing, or 'transforming', the conscious mind. If this understanding is accepted, the question still remains, however, as to the direction in which our minds are to be 'developed'. What skills, attitudes and values do we want developed in our children's minds? In what direction should their minds be 'transformed'?

In recent years it has become fashionable to regard children's formal education as largely concerned with developing those skills that are likely to prove most economically useful, both to the individual and to the British economy as a whole. Whilst lip service is paid to wider educational goals, the advent of the National Curriculum in British state schools has meant that the development of the wider aspects of children's awareness has often been neglected as more and more time is allocated to the pursuit of purely academic or vocational goals.

From a holistic perspective it would be acknowledged that education certainly needs to pay some attention to the demands of economic necessity.   Nevertheless, this entirely materialistic understanding of the purpose of education stresses only what might be termed the 'outer' aspects of humanity's purpose on earth. The demands of the body exist, and physical needs must undoubtedly be met, but from the point of view of holistic awareness, for this to be seen as education's only purpose, or even its major purpose, would be understood as a very limited conception of the role of education in developing our conscious minds.

iv. The nature of consciousness

Understanding the nature of consciousness is at the leading edge of much scientific research today, and considerable dispute exists between those who consider 'mind' as an almost accidental consequence of our physical bodies - a result of the physical connections between the neurones in our brains - and those who see it as something much more complex and subtle. The implications for education of our conception of 'mind' are considerable, for as Joan and Miroslav Borysenko point out in their book, *The Power of the Mind to Heal,* (Borysenko 1995):

> *"Those of us who believe that mind is a form of conscious awareness limited in space and time to the vicinity of our brain, subscribe to a paradigm, or belief system, resting on separation, isolation, and the ultimate finality of death. Those of us who believe that mind is a form of conscious awareness unlimited by space and time, and shared among all life ... subscribe to a paradigm of interconnectedness. "*

From a holistic point of view, 'mind' is understood from the perspective of this 'paradigm of interconnectedness', and the central task for education is therefore seen as that of developing each individual human mind to recognise and fulfil our parts in the life of a greater 'mind' - the mind of a greater 'whole' that is all creation.

As Alice Bailey (1987) has explained, the purpose of a holistic approach to education can therefore best be understood in terms of the expansion of the individual, ego-centred, consciousness towards that of the greater 'whole' . For from this perspective it is recognised that the purpose of education, like that of earthly life itself, is to be found in the evolution of personal consciousness to an awareness of that greater Mind of which we are all a part - the Mind of all that is.

v. The choice for education

In the upbringing of our children humanity has a choice. We may choose to develop in our children's minds the belief that the purely materialistic 'struggle for survival' is all that there is to life on earth. In which case, the resulting attitude of cut-throat competitive struggle will ensure that whilst a small proportion of children will 'succeed' in the education system, and go on to occupy well-paid responsible jobs, inevitably most will 'fail'. Those who fail are likely to be left with little to show from their years of formal education but the resentment, anger and despair that result from feeling that they have nothing of value to offer the world - no meaningful service they are capable of rendering in their community, no worthwhile gifts they can offer to humanity as a whole.

Alternatively, we may recognise that humanity's purpose on Earth is about more than mere 'survival', and that there is a greater consciousness than our individualised egos, and also a greater Life to fulfil than our personal share of the material cake. In which case we will come to understand that all individuals, no matter of what age, sex, race, or colour, have intrinsic worth as parts of that greater Life, and all have worthwhile gifts to offer, no matter how modest. The choice is entirely ours.

velopment

ourth criteria I have developed to define a holistic approach
ucation proposes that:

> *Education is a process of gradually unfolding*
> *development, which, in children, takes place in*
> *clearly defined stages*

i. A natural development plan

In his book *The Children on the Hill*, Michael Deakin, (1973),
relates the story of an extraordinary educational experiment. The
parents of the four children described in this book considered that
children have an innate urge to learn, and believed that if they
encouraged and supported their children in following their own
interests and enthusiasms they would develop quite naturally,
with no adult pressure, at a rate far beyond that normally
associated with our formal educational efforts. By the time the
book was written the eldest child was thirteen and was already
accepted as a mathematical genius who was in the process of
learning to use the massive central computer at Cambridge
University. The eight year old was a publicly acclaimed musician
who had won a piano-playing competition open to young people
twice his age, whilst both younger children already showed signs
of outstanding ability.

The ideas upon which this educational experiment was based are
also supported by those of Chilton Pearce, (1977). In his book,
The Magical Child, Pearce suggests that life has an innate
development plan for children, and that if adults encourage and
support them in following that inner plan, children's emotional
and intellectual capacities will develop as naturally as their
physical abilities.

An unswerving faith in the child's own natural powers of learning
was also the basis of Maria Montessori's educational work. She,
too, believed that children's intellectual and social development
will occur quite spontaneously if they are provided with a suitable
environment and supported in their learning process without
being overly controlled or directed. Indeed, she observed that if

children's own pattern of learning was respected, even very young children developed remarkable powers of concentration, and that the experience of this deep involvement with learning about the world appeared to have a remarkable effect also upon the children's attitude to life in general. After such an experience, she noted, children became more helpful and co-operative, serene and friendly. She termed this process the 'normalisation' of the child, and believed that it was a vital missing element in education in that the whole nature of the child appeared to be reassured and transformed by such deep learning experiences.

Holistic education is, therefore, based on the assumption that children naturally **want** to learn, and that if they are encouraged to learn in their own ways, and in their own time, they will not only be found to have immense potential that at present goes unrecognised, but are also likely to develop emotionally and socially as a result of their deeply involving educational experiences. Whilst many parents and teachers are likely to have grave misgivings about such an approach to education, arguing that children will never learn such 'essential' things as maths and grammar unless forced to do so, nevertheless considerable evidence from a variety of different sources now exists which supports the idea that children learn best when their learning is self-chosen and self-directed.

For example, one of the most extraordinarily successful nursery school projects, and one whose success is often quoted in support of the value of pre-school education, is based on a highly learner-directed approach to education. The High Scope pre-school programme was originally developed in Ypsilanti, Michigan, for children from severely socially disadvantaged families. The educational method developed for the project has been termed 'supported' learning by its originators. In this approach pre-school children are encouraged to choose and plan their own learning each day and to discuss with their teachers what they want to do and why. At the end of the day they again discuss with their teachers what they actually did, and whether they felt this was successful or not. This may seem an extraordinarily ambitious achievement for three and four year old children, and yet very long-term studies have followed the first intake of children to take part in this scheme into adult life.   These confirmed that, as adults, these children are not only more successful educationally than a control group of similar children, but are also much less likely to have committed crimes, are more likely to be in employment, to own their own home, and to have stable marriages, (Schweinhart, Barnes & Weikart, 1993).

In his famous book, *How Children Fail,* John Holt, (1984), has suggested that not only do children have this innate natural capacity for learning, but that the formal education system can` actually hamper and interfere with this natural learning process, and cause children to fail as learners when they would otherwise be perfectly competent.   This suggestion is supported by recent research which reports that whilst 82% of six year olds are confident of their ability to learn, this drops to only 18% of sixteen year olds, (Rose & Goll, 1992).

ii. Stages of development

Maria Montessori and Rudolf Steiner both considered that children's natural development takes place in three very different stages, and the theories proposed by these early pioneers of holistic education are supported by the work of the famous developmental psychologist, Jean Piaget.   Montessori and Steiner both suggested that in each stage of their development the focus of children's attention shifts from one aspect of their nature to another.   From birth to around six or seven years they considered children to be primarily focused on the mastery of their physical bodies and understanding the properties of their immediate physical environment. During the middle years of childhood this focus changes, and from around six or seven to the onset of adolescence at twelve to fourteen, both considered the main focus of children's learning to be on developing their emotional nature and an understanding of their social environment.   At puberty, the focus shifts again to the development of the mental aspect of their nature and only at this stage does an interest awaken in the theoretical principles and abstract forms of understanding that are the basis of most formal approaches to education.

iii. The physical stage: birth - 7 years

Montessori and Steiner both agreed that from birth to around six or seven years children's main focus of attention is on their physical development.   More recently, Jean Piaget, (1977), produced experimental evidence to support his view that the **intellectual** development of young children takes place largely as a result of their **physical** activity in the world. In other words, it is largely through their **physical** exploration of their environment that young children make sense of the world. Piaget's theories were the source of the "activity-based" approach to education introduced into British primary schools in the mid 1960s, where children are encouraged to learn through their own physical activities and active involvement in practical experiments. These methods have aroused considerable controversy, and have been much criticised recently by those who would prefer to see more emphasis placed on the skills of literacy and numeracy, which they consider to be the 'basics' of a sound education. Whilst further research is clearly needed before any definite conclusions can be drawn, nevertheless the current political trend to discredit the activity-based approach to learning and reinstate formal intellectual educational methods, may well prove counter-productive if further research supports these theories.

iv. The emotional stage: 7 - 14 years

Later stages of childhood development are even less clearly understood than this first early stage, but from a holistic perspective it would be suggested that from around six or seven until puberty, children are mainly focused on developing their emotional nature. This they do largely through imaginative play with other children, creating social and situational dramas in which to live out their emotional interactions and reactions.

Children's fantasy play also serves an important role in developing their powers of creative imagination. Psychology is only just beginning to appreciate the extraordinary power of the human mind; but from a holistic view it is understood that the mind is humanity's most crucial creative tool. As children in the middle years of childhood absorb themselves for endless hours in games of 'make believe', they are not 'just playing', as we so often dismiss this apparently pointless activity, but are in fact exercising the natural tool they have been given to develop their powers of creative imagination.

The rapid growth of children's emotional and behavioural difficulties in recent years is at last beginning to focus attention on children's emotional development, but their need for support in developing emotional awareness and control is still largely ignored in the formal education system. As adults we are clearly aware that emotional distress can have a seriously inhibiting effect on our ability to learn, and in his best-selling book, *Emotional Intelligence,* Daniel Goleman, (1996), provides substantial evidence to support his view that our capacity to deal successfully with our emotions - our 'emotional intelligence' - is a more accurate predictor of success in life than academic achievement. Nevertheless, as Alice Miller, (1987), has pointed out, we still do not take children's emotions seriously, and often relate to them in ways we would never dream of treating an adult. Nor do we provide children with any substantial information or understanding in the realm of human emotions - indeed such matters are rarely discussed during their formal education and our emotional responses are treated almost as a taboo subject in schools. Emotional 'control' is somehow expected to arise 'naturally', fully developed and perfectly functional, without children ever being given the opportunity to acknowledge or discuss their feelings in the public context of their schooling. Even the issue of parenting - a vitally important social activity which will be part of the life experience of almost all human beings - is largely ignored in our formal education system, and young people are expected to develop these essential skills purely on the basis of natural 'instincts'. If there is one area of our present education system that needs attention more urgently than any other, it is perhaps our complete neglect of children's emotional development, and our refusal to acknowledge their desperate needs in this area.

v. The mental stage: 14 years onwards

From a holistic perspective it would be suggested that it is only as children reach adolescence that they develop the capacity to think in terms of the abstract intellectual logic that is the basis of our formal education system. Indeed, recent research in America, (Gardner, 1993), suggests that there are many different types of intelligence, and that the rational intellectual approach to learning that is the basis of most formal education systems may be quite unsuited to the individual learning styles of large numbers of adults also. Gardner also provides evidence to show that even those young people who are considered 'successful' in terms of their formal education, are often quite unable to make use of the information they have apparently mastered in any context other than formal tests, and that therefore their knowledge can in no real sense be considered of genuine use to them - a failing of the formal academic education system also pointed out by John Holt.

From a holistic perspective it is recognised that since children naturally **want** to learn, they will learn most effectively if their innate learning pattern is respected, supported and encouraged and they are given opportunities to learn through their own self-directed experience. Adults can best support children's learning by offering encouragement for this natural learning process, and by providing the resources and support that will help children to integrate their learning within their unfolding understanding of the holistic nature of reality.

5. Love

The fifth criteria of holistic education proposes that:

> *The nature of the universal Spirit is love, and the development of loving consciousness is central to successful education.*

i. Love and education

I once watched a television programme where the issue of children being sent to boarding school was being discussed. It followed the progress of a group of quite young children as they were being sent away to school, and then interviewed some adults who had themselves been sent to boarding school as children. One of these adults described the terrible sense of isolation from, and rejection by, his family, that he had experienced when he had been sent away to school as a young child. The emotional pain and grief that he still carried from the experience as an adult were almost palpable through the television screen. He suggested that whilst boarding schools might provide any number of excellent educational 'facilities', what they did not, and could not, provide, was love.

Although it is extremely difficult to measure and prove objectively, considerable evidence now exists to suggest that whether or not a child feels loved, particularly by their parents and immediate family, is of crucial importance to their 'performance' in the formal education system. This is perhaps most obvious at the extremes, but it is likely that it also applies at more subtle levels. Nevertheless, it is particularly obvious that children who are beaten and ill-treated, who are sexually abused, or whose parents are drug-addicted or alcoholic, are hardly likely to 'perform' well in formal education.

To compare the educational achievements of such children - and they are many - with those from comfortable secure middle class homes with devoted intelligent parents who work hard to ensure that their children's needs are properly met, is grossly unfair both to the children themselves, and to those teachers who care enough about such children to be prepared to struggle against all the odds to help them - often in under-resourced inner city schools with a high preponderance of children with major life problems.

Yet this is precisely what is now being done when politicians talk of 'not making excuses' for poor performance in education because of children's social background. Research evidence certainly demonstrates that well organised schooling, particularly good education in the early years, can make a substantial difference to children's academic achievements, (Mortimer et. al., 1988). Nevertheless international research results confirm again and again that it is the level of ability children demonstrate when they first arrive at school that will determine the major differences in their long-term achievements in their formal education. In other words, it is the quality of the child's experience in their homes, **before** they ever attend formal school, that largely determines their long-term success or failure in the education system. For no amount of 'structured' learning or 'proper' discipline in school can ever make up to a child for not being loved and cared for by their own family.

ii. The psychology of love

Whilst still largely ignored in the formal education system, the importance of love to the development of human personality is now increasingly widely acknowledged in psychology.   In his book, *The Road Less Travelled,* the American psychiatrist Scott Peck, (1987), proposes a theory that the human response to love is the fundamental basis of all psychological development. Without it, he suggests, the development of human personality is likely to be as warped and stunted as our physical development becomes when deprived of essential nutrition.   Similar conclusions were reached by John Bowlby, (1965), one of this century's major developmental psychologists.   He proposed that the strength of children's emotional bonds of attachment to their parents forms the basis of all later mental and emotional health.   His research with young children who had been institutionalised at an early age revealed that if these bonds were broken too suddenly, and no new attachment could be established, such children were likely to be emotionally damaged for life.   It is now widely acknowledged that children who have been in institutional care make up a very high proportion of the criminal population.

In a study of a South American tribe living in the Amazon forests, Jean Liedloff, (1979), explains how she too came to the conclusion that close loving contact, particularly physical contact, with their parents and other adults, is of crucial importance to children's later emotional health.   She suggests that if this early need is met, children are far more likely to develop into emotionally stable and psychologically resilient adults.   Her ideas are supported by evidence from animal studies, which have shown that if baby monkeys are deprived of close physical contact with their mothers they grow up psychologically insecure and socially inept.   They are also more likely to develop serious physical illness because such early separation appears to result in the suppression of the immune system, (Siegel ,1988).

iii. The universal spirit

From a holistic perspective, the crucial importance of love in human development is understood as an inevitable outcome of the centrality of love in the universe. Children come into the world with an emotional system 'programmed' to receive nourishment through love, just as our physical bodies are adapted to accept physical nourishment from food . For love is understood as the essential nature of the universal spirit, and all life's many forms are recognised as parts of this single universal being. The parts of this universal energy flow are inherently attractive to one another, because essentially all are one. In the physical world the attractive power between apparently separate objects is understood in terms of electro-magnetic energy fields or the force of gravity, but as human beings we experience it as the power of 'love'.

The spiritual traditions of most of the world's major religions also acknowledge the central importance of love; and in the Christian tradition it is understood as the essential nature of the relationship between humanity and the Creator. In a well known passage from John's Gospel in The New Testament, we are told:

> *"Beloved, let us love one another: for love is of God; and every one that loveth is born of God, and knoweth God. He that loveth not knoweth not God; for God is love."*

> John Ch. 4 v. 7-8

The place of love in the tradition of an historical group known as the Essenes, by whom it seems possible that Jesus was educated during his years in the desert as a child, is summarised by Edmond Bordeaux Szekely, (1976), when he says:

> *"Love was considered by the Essenes to be the highest creative feeling and they held that a cosmic ocean of love exists everywhere uniting all forms of life, and that life itself is an expression of love."*

The same understanding underlies the work of many of today's spiritual teachers. In *Choosing to Love,* Eileen Caddy and David Earl Platts, (1993), of the Findhorn Foundation stress the centrality of love to personal relationships when they explain that:

> *"Love is the indescribable, powerful energy flowing through our whole being out to all our fellow men and women, enabling us to see beyond their outer form to the divinity within each one, creating within us a feeling of oneness, wholeness and "the peace of God which passes all understanding."*

In her bestselling book, *Living with Joy*, (1986), the well-known writer Sanaya Roman also accepts the centrality of love, for as she explains:

> *"Love is the food of the universe. It is the most important ingredient of life. Children go towards love, they thrive on love and grow on love and would die without it. Love is an energy that circles the world; it exists everywhere and in everything."*

iv. Values

Shortly after my daughter started her 'A' level course at our local College of Further Education, I recall her coming home one evening and recounting with considerable indignation the story of a lecturer's behaviour in class that day, and his attitude to some spelling mistakes she had made in her work. *"He tried to humiliate me in front of the whole class, Mum,"* she said, *"- and he did it **deliberately!**"* I burst out laughing in amazement and delight at the fact that a girl of seventeen had no previous experience of this 'disciplinary' technique. *"Why do you think I kept you out of school all these years?"* I asked.

For even at that early stage of my understanding of education, I was aware that it is essential for children to feel that they are loved and valued by the adults around them if they are to develop the healthy sense of self-esteem that we now recognise to be essential to success in formal education. Like many of us, I can recall all too clearly from my personal experience at school the terrible emotional suffering the technique of deliberately humiliating children can cause. Self-esteem is, of course a complex phenomenon, and children whose families love and value them for themselves are unlikely to be as easily damaged by the unwitting cruelty of teachers employing such techniques as those whose self-worth is already fragile.   Nevertheless such attitudes to children raise important questions as to the values which teachers communicate, often unconsciously, to the children in our schools.

Whilst politicians pontificate about the importance of teaching children 'right from wrong', research clearly demonstrates that it is what children see done in practice by the adults around them that will most effectively influence their moral standards. So if we wish our children to grow up as respectful, caring adults, able to both fulfil their individual potential and form successful relationships with others, we must first demonstrate such values in the way we as adults relate both to our children and to one another.   It is pointless bemoaning the increase of violent disrespectful behaviour amongst children, if we ourselves, and the media images with which our children are constantly surrounded, portray adult life as concerned only with our own 'survival' or 'success', indifferent to the suffering of others and with the art of the vicious 'put down' accepted as clever and 'cool'. We as adults need to demonstrate a moral choice in the values by which we live our own lives. Is it 'survival of the fittest' or 'love your neighbour as yourself'? For as Jesus explained nearly 2000 years ago: *"No man can serve two masters"*.

From a holistic perspective, a spirit of love and respect for the innate value and worth of all children, regardless of their particular gifts or achievements, is understood as the essence of education. For from this perspective it is understood that love is the essential nature of the Universal Spirit, and gives inner meaning and purpose to all our lives. Without it there can be no true learning, no truly human growth or development. For love is the essential nature of the Holy Spirit, and only if our earthly lives reflect this understanding in practice do we ourselves become truly human.

6. Creativity

I have defined the sixth criteria of a holistic approach to education in terms of:

Self-chosen creative expression is vital to educational development.

According to recent research, few teachers are conscious of children as innately creative. Whilst they often value creativity, they tend to see it as exceptional - a 'rare gift'. From a holistic perspective, however, creativity is understood as the essential nature of the Universal Spirit, and consequently the essential nature also of all human beings.

In the past, schooling was designed to prepare the majority of young people for the repetitive, tedious, uncreative work available in factories and offices. Whilst a small elite might go on to "better things" through higher education, most were destined to service the machines of the factory age. Today more and more of this mind-numbingly tedious work is being taken over by computers and robots, freeing human beings for the more intelligent and creative aspects of work. A life of creative freedom has been humanity's dream throughout history, but in the past it was achievable only by the wealthy few at the expense of the impoverished masses who were either used as slaves, or employed as servants or machine minders, thus freeing the wealthy for a life of creative leisure. Many social commentators are warning that we are now living at the start of an age when those who will be best fitted to earn a living will be those who are flexible, adaptable, and creative. For the days of thousands of workers employed on the treadmills of the industrial machine are gone. Those who will earn a good living in the 21st Century will be those with creative imagination as well as skills and self-discipline. So whilst our education system continues to train young people for an age that has already gone - an age of mass employment in routine work - employers search for those who can innovate and think creatively. Today's education will grossly fail our children if it fails to empower their creativity.

i. Creative freedom

From a holistic perspective, however, creative self-expression is not seen to be of value only because of its potential to help us earn a living in the economic conditions prevailing at the start of a new century. For the individual's freedom to follow their own creative path in life is seen as essential to the full flowering of our human talents and abilities.

The extraordinary results of allowing children creative freedom are revealed in an account of the development of the Harriana School in Egypt, (Wissa Wassef, 1972). Here the founder of the school describes how he devised an experiment to test his belief that all human beings are innately creative, and that our formal education, particularly in the field of art, all too often serves only to destroy this innate creative talent. Wissa Wassef set up a small weaving workshop in a village just outside Cairo where he taught a group of local peasant children the basic skill of weaving. Once the children had mastered the simple techniques involved in operating the looms, he deliberately taught them nothing further about the art and craft of weaving. Instead, he provided them with all the necessary materials, and left them free to develop their own skills and forms of artistic expression. This group of totally uneducated peasant children created such magnificent works of art that their tapestries are now world famous and exhibited in major galleries world-wide.

ii. Freedom or anarchy?

Whilst creative freedom in education is recognised as an essential key to children's development, there has undoubtedly been much confusion around the issue. For as we ourselves discovered when we offered our children out of school a totally unstructured education, the concept of creative freedom has often been misunderstood. Too frequently it has been interpreted to mean that structure and discipline are unnecessary in human life, but as any creative artist knows, this is very far from the truth. Nevertheless, the issue of how far children should be given 'freedom' in their lives has plagued both modern psychology and attempts to introduce more 'progressive' approaches to education.

The concept of creative freedom has too often been misinterpreted as meaning children's right to do what ever they want, regardless of the effects of their behaviour on other people. This is not at all the same thing as **creative** freedom, but merely an encouragement to out and out selfishness. Self-centred anarchy, and the right to exercise our human creative freedom, need to be disentangled in our understanding of what is meant by "freedom" in education. Expecting children to behave with some sense of consideration for the rights and needs of others does not involve the destruction of their right to be themselves, nor of their inner creative potential.

A balanced solution to these recurring educational dilemmas has been suggested by one of this century's greatest educators - the Brazilian, Paulo Freire, (1972). He proposed the concept of an educational 'dialogue' between learners and those who aim to support and encourage their learning. This involves both parties as equal partners in the learning process, and each is understood to be entitled to air their views and be heard by the other. Much evidence now suggests that where learners are involved in such a process, the results of their learning are substantially better than when this is directed entirely by those with authority over them.

From a holistic perspective, therefore, whilst the necessity for structure, organisation and discipline are clearly recognised, they are understood as the need to support and encourage children's **self** discipline and **self** organisation, not as encouragement to the arbitrary imposition of incomprehensible 'rules' by external authority.

iii. Creativity or art?

It is politically fashionable today to deride the value of personal creativity, and to suggest that unless what is created is of outstanding cultural merit, it has no real worth. From a holistic perspective, however, it is recognised that our personal acts of creation can be of very considerable educational value, regardless of whether they would be culturally regarded as 'art'. For it is understood that the very act of creation itself often produces insights which the learner would not otherwise obtain. In my own experience as a learner I have made use of personal journals, or 'Portfolios'. Whilst I would not wish to claim these as standing within our cultural tradition as great works of art, there is no doubt in my own mind that I have learnt a great deal through keeping them. Indeed, they have been of crucial importance to me in both my personal growth as a human being, and in the development of my understanding of education.

iv. The creative impulse

Whilst there is still considerable argument in academic circles as to the ultimate source of the creative impulse, many highly creative people acknowledge that their creativity does not arise from deliberate acts of their own will, but from remaining open to that mysterious inner light of inspiration which has its source in the greater 'whole' that is all creation.

From a holistic perspective it is recognised that the nature of the one life is essentially creative, and individual creativity can therefore be understood as a reflection of the creative nature of the universal spirit. Each individualised part of the whole is seen to have its own gifts and talents - its own particular expressions of the creative attributes of the universal life. The creative impulse within each of us is therefore recognised as a guiding light which leads us on to fulfil our maximum potential.

The particular gift of the universal Spirit to the human species is that of 'free will' - we are free to choose our own forms of self-expression. From a holistic perspective, therefore, creative self-expression is understood as one of humanity's greatest gifts. For in the exercise of our creative impulses lies the path of our most profound growth and learning as a human being. When we are forced by parents, teachers, or society at large, to ignore our own inner creative impulses, we begin to deny and lose touch with our own most central learning opportunities, and these may never be recovered. This is not only an individual tragedy, but a collective calamity for all humanity.

From a holistic perspective therefore, it is recognised that our personal creativity is not a luxury to be indulged if we have time and energy at the end of a busy working week, but an essential element of our growth, both individually and as a species.

7. Spiritual

The last criterion of a holistic approach to education is, perhaps, the most important, but it is also the least familiar to modern rationalist thought, for it suggest that:

Holistic education aims to empower the individual to walk their own life path in a conscious effort to fulfil their particular part in the spiritual whole that is all Life.

The idea that as individuals we are integral parts of a greater 'whole', which has a purpose in our creation, is fundamental to the spiritual view of reality. As such, it is understood that in earthly life the task for each individual is to discover and fulfil the purpose that the greater Life has in their creation. For as Paulo Coelho, (1995), explains in his beautiful fable *The Alchemist*:

> *"When you really want something, it's because that desire originated in the soul of the universe. It's your mission on earth ... To realise one's destiny is a person's only real obligation."*

During my studies for a master's degree one of the observation days I spent with a London middle school involved a day out at a farm in the country. I was particularly interested in the response of one child to this experience, for in the classroom this boy was apathetic and slow, and obviously unlikely to be a high achiever in academic terms. He also had a tendency to be something of a trouble maker, and was clearly not popular with his class teacher.

As the children wandered around the arable farm we visited in the morning, the boy showed no signs of any particular interest in the visit, and the fact that he was quite seriously overweight made the long walk round arable fields an arduous exercise for him. In the afternoon, however, we arrived at a dairy farm, and as we entered the yards where the animals were kept, this child's whole attitude transformed. He became lively, excited and animated, asked questions continuously, and was the first to put up his hand to answer them. A brief mention of a technical word during the early part of the visit had obviously been clearly remembered later in the day when this boy was the first to answer the question, *"What do the cows eat in the winter?"* *"Silage",* came the instantaneous reply from this child. As we walked back to our coach I asked the lad if he had enjoyed the visit. His face shone with delight as he told me he had. *"Would you like to work on a farm?"* I asked him. *"Yea!"* he affirmed unequivocally.

This young boy obviously had a deep affinity with animals - particularly with cows, and if his education had been my responsibility, almost everything he did from that point on would have been related to farming, and farm animals. For from the boy's excitement and interest in the animals, and the transformation their presence created in his attitude to life, it was clear to me that his higher purpose in life involved contact with animals in some form - possibly only as a humble stockman - but then does the world not need stockmen just as much as it needs brain surgeons?

For me this incident represented a fascinating example of one of the most important underlying spiritual principles of a holistic approach to education: the concept that as individuals we are integral parts of a greater 'whole', which has a purpose in our being here on Earth.   The task for education is therefore to empower us to fulfil our highest purpose on earth - the part that has been designed for us in the 'whole' that is all creation.

In one of my entries in my Portfolios I describe my own understanding of the concept of a higher purpose in our individual lives, and the importance of this concept to education, when I explain that:

> " This is what is so totally fascinating about following one's true "life purpose". For in following that path and in developing one's true work, lie the most potent of Life's "lessons" for the individual soul. Here lies the true path of the soul's evolution and growth."

> "It is this element of self-directed education that is so terribly difficult to explain to those who do not understand the spiritual nature of the educational process. For only if one recognises the soul of the individual as a co-creator of their own lives, in conscious co-operation with the greater "Mind-of-all-that-is", can one begin to understand how crucial it is for each soul to follow their own true purpose - their own "Life Path", along which the Great Spirit has, in the

*sheer perfection and brilliance of the design of
the "whole" of creation, laid out the soul's most
important life "lessons" and evolutionary
"tasks"..."*

From a holistic perspective our earthly lives are understood as
mirrors of our consciousness - mirrors that are designed to help us
recognise our own inner spiritual nature and to understand our
spiritual destiny on earth. Like the mirrors of a kaleidoscope
reflecting each small piece of coloured material to create a greater
pattern, our individual lives are reflected in the mirror of the
greater 'whole'. If these lives are off course, or out of alignment,
so too will the pattern we see in the mirror of our own lives be a
distorted one. Like dancers in a chorus line, or formation team,
who are out of line, the mirror of our earthly life will reflect that
lack of understanding of our spiritual destiny on earth - our
success or failure in walking our spiritual path and our conscious
co-operation in fulfilling our higher purpose on earth.

From a holistic perspective it is therefore recognised that the
process of education cannot be properly understood if it is seen
only as acquiring information about the material world, or
physical or vocational skills. For education ultimately involves
the development of our ability to recognise and fulfil our personal
spiritual destiny. The ultimate aim of a holistic approach to
education can thus be understood as a means to empower the
individual to walk their own life path, with a conscious desire to
fulfil their part in the spiritual Whole that is all Life.

This concept of education is not one that is easily understood in
our materialistic society, nor one that is widely reflected in our
present methods of schooling. It is nevertheless a central
principle of a holistic approach, and our failure to understand its
importance is seen as the heart of education's malaise.

For children who are given no sense of conscious understanding
of their greater purpose in life are like explorers without a
compass - they lack any sense of direction. Material, social, or
financial 'success' can offer but a poor substitute for inner
meaning to their lives - that inner fulfilment that comes only

from the achievement of our true life purpose. But whilst children and young people often sense this lack, our society offers few tools to help them understand the nature of their loss, and all too many that merely confuse and distract.

In writing in my Portfolio, I considered my own feelings about our society's restricted understanding of humanity's purpose on earth, and of the difficulties this creates both for education itself, and for me personally, when I wrote:

"I long with all my soul to communicate to the children what I have learnt so painfully in this difficult lifetime. I long to communicate it also to the adults that they may not repeat their own mistakes upon the children once more. At last I begin to understand that awful statement in the Bible about the sins of the fathers being visited upon the children - even unto the third and fourth generation. Indeed we do!"

"Yet I find the task of this communication so difficult, for the very terms in which it is comprehensible are not yet accepted or understood by society as a whole."

"How can I discuss the importance of manifesting in the outer symbolic world of forms, the inner meaning and truth of reality? How can I explain the deadly importance of a little scenario I watched on BBC Children's TV the other day? The attractive young black presenter with his idiotic squawking duck obviously had absolutely no idea of the psychic damage he was unconsciously doing the children. Yet after showing a sweet little film about an elephant who ran away, but ended up returning to her friends who all told her how much they loved her, this presenter commented to the viewers: 'Love?' and then demonstrated his attitude by pretending to be sick!"

"What can I say? How can I ever explain that he is teaching the children to deny the most important spiritual reality of their inner world ..."

"How can I ever explain my philosophy of education, when the values of this civilization do not even recall the most basic of all spiritual values?   How can I say that it is utterly essential that children's education is rooted in a conscious understanding of the importance of love to their development when our civilization itself doesn't understand the importance and value of love?"

"How can I ever explain to the world that children need to have their inner reality confirmed in the outer world, or else they will become split and disorientated.   Driven to accept the values exhibited in the outer world in order to find love and acceptance in that world; but in the process forced to deny their innermost truth and cut off from the one Source of inner guidance, inspiration and truth that could lead them back to some semblance of understanding of their lives and conflicts, and some attempt at resolution."

"It fills me with horror to see what is being done to the children psychically at this time.   And then we wonder why they are hooligans at 5; criminals at 8; and drug addicts at 11."

"This society, its values, and its "education" system are systematically destroying our children - yet we do not understand what we are doing.   To attempt to explain it means I have also to attempt to explain a whole different value system, a whole different approach to life, a whole psychic and spiritual world which is largely beyond the comprehension of our "civilized" consciousness."

"No wonder I sometimes feel daunted by the task! However it is the task I have been set by the One - the task the Great Spirit seems to have appointed as my particular work on Earth.   So I must begin, and simply trust that God will help me with what appears to be impossible."

"I take great comfort these days, as the darkness closes ever deeper upon the consciousness of human-kind, in Christ's words:

"For men it is impossible, but not for God; everything is possible for God"

Mark 10 v. 27.

Chapter three

Future possibilities

If we are to meet the educational needs of young people at this time the development of practical options for a more holistic approach to education is an urgent priority. Undoubtedly, the options that eventually emerge will be many and various, for whilst the principles of a holistic approach to education are likely to remain constant, there is a variety of methods through which these could be applied. In this section, however, I will examine in some detail two practical developments which are being actively pursued at the present time.   Whilst they are still in their embryonic stages, these could provide the basis for complementary initiatives for the future.

1. The Education Centre

We have come to accept that 'education' takes place in some kind of institution. Be it a 'school' or a 'college', we tend to visualise education taking place at a fixed location, where those being educated attend on a regular basis. In his book, *De-schooling Society,* Ivan Illich, (1971), proposed an alternative model for education. In the 'deschooled society' Illich suggested, children and young people would no longer learn in the confined environment of a school or college classroom, but would have access to learning in a wide variety of settings in the local community.

In mainstream education today, 'distance learning' is becoming an increasingly important concept. Here the learner studies mainly at home, or out on a work placement, attends few, if any, formal classes or lectures, and links up with their tutors at their college or other educational centre for periodic meetings or seminars, either face to face or through video-conferencing facilities.

Students are also likely to submit regular written work for assessment. The Open University is probably the best known model for distance learning in Britain today, but many new initiatives are in the process of being developed, such as the proposed new University of the Highlands and Islands where a number of existing colleges are being linked to distance learners through the latest information technology.

This highly flexible new model for education is largely confined to adult learners at present; for it clearly poses certain difficulties with very young children who need adults not only to support their learning, but also to take care of them. We will examine a proposed solution for younger children when we discuss the second possible model for holistic education - Education in Community. For the moment, however, the flexible learning option appears quite realistic for young people in the 14+ stage of their education.

Each major Education Centre would be located in a large city, and this would serve as the educational base for its particular area, rather as Colleges of Further Education do today. Such a centre would act as an administrative and resource base, but each centre would also be likely to have a number of subsidiary centres where possible specialist activities could take place. The centre would also be likely to offer access to a wide network of other groups and projects which would provide the basis for education to take place in the surrounding community. Instead of travelling long distances by bus or train to attend classes each day, as many students at schools and colleges have to do today, the education centres would develop an individual educational programme for each student, based on their own particular interests and enthusiasms. This would enable them to study at home, from a work-experience placement, or from a placement with a voluntary project.

Each student would probably attend the centre for an initial assessment course, during which they would establish a relationship with the personal tutor who would support and direct their study programme. They would also become a member of a small study team -a group of students who would continue to meet up together at regular intervals throughout their period of study at the centre to offer support and a social context for learning.

Perhaps we can best understand how this idea could work in practice by following the progress of two imaginary students. Let us say that they are near neighbours in their homes and have known each other since primary school. After the younger - a girl we shall call Sarah - decides to join such an Education Centre, her friend and near neighbour, whom we will call Tom, also decides that such a centre might be able to help him with his educational difficulties.

Sarah is a highly gifted child. She has a measured IQ score of around 160, (ie. over half as much again as the 'average', which is defined as 100). Sarah has been reading since she was three years old, but despite her brilliant gifts she has had persistent difficulties at the local schools she has attended.

Her first teacher, a well-meaning but desperately over-worked woman, with a reception class of over 30 children, largely ignored Sarah. She saw her task as a teacher as ensuring that all the many children in her care got a thorough grounding in 'the basics'. Sarah could already read and write fluently, and was also well ahead of her classmates in her number work. So her teacher saw her as 'all right'. She did not need her teachers over-stretched time and energy as much as other, less able, children.

Sarah did not mind at first. The new environment of school was quite interesting, and she enjoyed playing with the other children. Her primary school was 'activity based' and she was allowed considerable freedom to choose her own activities from amongst the range of good quality equipment available in her classroom. She coped well.

As Sarah progressed up the school, however, her education gradually became more formal. She never had any problems with the work required of her, but she was constantly bored. No special provision was made for her exceptional gifts - indeed when her parents discussed this option with one of her later teachers he dismissed it out of hand as unnecessary, and contrary to the schools 'equal opportunities' policy.

Both Sarah and her parents became increasingly frustrated and distressed. A private visit to an educational psychologist confirmed the truth of her exceptional gifts. The psychologist's report was handed to the Head Teacher, and meetings arranged to discuss Sarah's exceptional needs. But still no action resulted.

Sarah's exceptional academic abilities marked her out at school as 'different' and she had few close friends. She started to withdraw into herself, and became increasingly introverted and unhappy. Her academic work also started to deteriorate, and by the time Sarah started at secondary school she no longer shone academically. Her work was 'above average', but there was no apparent justification for any 'exceptional needs' teaching as far as the school could identify.

Whilst she remained something of an isolate and nonentity at school, at home Sarah continued to pursue her real passion - environmental studies. Sarah's parents ran a smallholding and her real life revolved around the animals, plants and wild life of her home base. Increasingly frequently Sarah would plead 'sick' first thing in the morning. Her concerned parents would release her from a day's schooling, only to realise that by mid-morning she was happily mucking-out her pony!

As they tried to put pressure on Sarah to attend school more regularly, however, she became increasingly rebellious, and after several months they discovered that she was a persistent truant, preferring to spend her days sitting alone with a book in the local cemetery to attending her hated school.

Her desperate parents began to cast around for other options for Sarah's education, and came across some information about a new Education Centre in their local town. At a stage where they were prepared to try almost anything that offered some hope for Sarah's future, they arranged an initial interview.

Sarah was reluctant; but after she discovered that here she would be allowed, indeed encouraged, to focus her academic work around her fascination with environmental issues, she quickly agreed to attend a 'summer school' which would act as her initial assessment course. If she and her parents decided that it was right for her to attend the Centre as a full-time student, she would then be in a position to begin her full-time studies at the beginning of the Autumn term instead of returning to school.

In her chosen field Sarah shone immediately. In the autumn she became a full-time student at the Centre, and from then on her time was mostly spent at home on her parents smallholding, although she attended the centre once a week to discuss her work with her personal tutor, and meet with her study group.

However most of her time was spent working on her personal research project.   Entitled, 'The Ecology of a Wiltshire Smallholding', it was a detailed study of her parents organic holding. She was thus able to spend long hours happily observing and recording the plants and wild life of her immediate surroundings, and research in depth the advantages and difficulties of organic husbandry.

Inspired in more formal academic work by being allowed to follow her real interests and enthusiasms, Sarah is also able to complete successfully a range of GCSE subjects and go on to A level work recognising that she will need such formal qualifications in order to pursue her real love at University and beyond.

One of Sarah's longest-standing friends is a local boy we have called Tom. Since early childhood they have shared their interest in animals and plants, and this has held together an otherwise somewhat unlikely friendship. Tom is nearly four years older than Sarah, and at eighteen he has abandoned full-time schooling with no formal academic qualifications. Like Sarah, Tom's interest is in animals and the natural world, and he has been trying to obtain work as a stockman on a local farm without success. His hopes of securing a training placement on a farm were also dashed, and, reluctantly, he has been forced to accept a training place with a local food-processing firm instead. After a year with this firm he is frustrated and bored, and, in the company of some other local 'lads', has started to drink too much.

Sarah is concerned for her long-time friend, and suggests he ask his parents if he too could become a student at the Education Centre she is attending. His parents are unwilling. They have little money to spare, and want Tom to get a full-time job as quickly as possible. Sarah persists, however, and suggests that Tom apply for a bursary to attend the Centre, which he receives after attending for a week-end's initial assessment course.

In discussion with his personal tutor it is agreed that Tom is not particularly interested in pursuing an academic career, and that his hopes for his long-term future are centred on farming. Tom's educational work with the Centre lies mainly in the area of developing his personal life management skills - learning how to set his own goals, how to plan realistic objectives for achieving those goals; and where to find the support he needs to realise his aim of work as a stockman.

After Tom completes his government-sponsored training placement with the food processing firm, he manages to secure a further work experience placement which the Centre arranges for him on a dairy farm in Dorset. Here he will be part of a small group of young people who live on the farm for extended periods, and, in return for their labour, receive their board and lodging, and some pocket money, as well as a basic training in dairy farming. Tom has begun his work placement, which he is enjoying, and is at last on his way towards a career in animal husbandry.

2. Education in Community

Whilst distance and flexible learning in Centres of Education may provide suitable models for the education of older children, what of the younger ones? For younger children the options of work placements, active involvement with community-based projects, or distance learning, are clearly more difficult to develop. Young children require more continuous support for their learning, and their safety and physical needs must also be taken into account during the years of their education. For these younger children another solution will therefore be needed.

There is a traditional African saying which claims that: *'It takes a whole village to educate a child',* and this could perhaps suggest a possible solution to the dilemma of how best to develop practical options for the education of younger children.

The most usual pattern for human social organisation in pre-industrial societies all over the world has been the village. The extended families of up to a dozen adults which form the most basic unit of human society rarely live in isolation, but join together in groups of between fifty and two or three hundred adults, so that they are able to fulfil those basic physical tasks necessary to human survival in co-operation, as well as enjoy the social and emotional pleasures of a variety of human companions.

The often dangerous tasks of hunting and fishing for food were frequently undertaken by the men of the village together in communal groups whereas caring for the children was more frequently done by the women.   As these basic tasks were superseded by more complex agricultural and industrial processes, however, these male dominated groups gradually developed a brilliant organisational structure of their own. Called the limited liability company, it quickly attained a legal status not possessed by either the family or the village community group. This formal recognition of their purpose by the wider society has enabled limited companies to develop enormous wealth and power. But instead of using this power to serve the needs of the whole community of which they are a part, these new companies have become increasingly self-seeking, using their enormous power simply to make profits for their shareholders. Thus the original communal purpose of the male hunting group - that of serving the interests of the family and community as a whole - has been replaced by a motive which seeks to serve no other purpose than maximising the success of the group itself.

More and more younger families are beginning to recognise that a lifestyle that is subservient to the aim of maximising corporate profit does not meet the needs of their families, and are seeking instead to develop lifestyles in small scale community groups. For they are coming to understand that such human-scale groups are much more suited to meeting the needs of human beings when these are viewed from a holistic perspective. For whilst the limited liability company is undoubtedly a brilliant organisational tool to meet what has historically been the essentially male purpose of providing the family with food and shelter, such groups are structurally inadequate for the task of meeting the needs of women with children, or the family as a whole.

It is now widely understood by modern psychology that children respond best in intimate, small-scale groups whose size does not overwhelm them. Such groups not only provide children with the physical security it is becoming increasingly difficult for the inherently unstable nuclear family to offer, but they also gain the emotional security of being known **personally** to a variety of adults of all ages, who also provide them with a wide selection of adult role models.   Neither the mass media, nor interactive computers, can make up for such personal relationships which are essential to children's healthy mental and emotional development.

There is, therefore, a wide-spread international movement today which aims to develop lifestyles that are more appropriate to the needs of the family in the form of new small-scale communities. These are not the 'communes' that flourished in the sixties, but tend towards a village form of organisation where each individual or family has their own home and garden, yet where major natural and productive resources are communally owned and managed.

Whilst   ardent   'free-marketeers'   may   argue   that   common ownership of land is incompatible with individual private enterprise, from a holistic perspective it would be argued that the economics of untrammelled private enterprise, are based on an unquestioned, but essentially flawed, assumption that it is possible to create a free and fair 'market' whilst there is an unequal right of access to that most basic of all natural resources - the land itself. Such a fundamental inequality creates a serious imbalance in the market, since this is a resource that cannot be created by any human endeavour. From the perspective of a more sustainable approach to economics it can be seen that this most fundamental resource of nature has rightfully been bestowed equally upon the whole of humanity. Indeed, the land itself needs to be understood as the property of the even wider community of Life - human, animal and plant - and should be managed in accordance with the principles of natural justice.

In the new villages, the community as a whole is also likely to own other shared resources: community buildings, educational buildings, and industrial and commercial premises, for example. These are also administered for the benefit of all community members, but may be leased out to individuals wishing to make use of them for their personal benefit. In which case the rental income still accrues to the benefit of the group as a whole. This aspect of community economics is already working well in a number of community enterprise schemes, and provides for a balance of both individual freedom and initiative and the interests of the community as a whole. Such communities are also more likely to aim to manage their resources on a sustainable basis, since this is clearly in the group's long-term interests.

Such small scale communities also provide an ideal setting for the development of new models of a holistic approach to education, and the children's education is likely to be one of their highest priorities.

An education resource centre would probably be amongst the communally owned buildings, and it is also likely that there would a special centre for younger children. These centres would be staffed throughout the day by the community's education workers, who would either be paid for their services by the community as a whole, or whose work at one of the education centres would form part of the community service commitment of individual members to the group as a whole. The children would be free to come and go from the education centres as they chose, and would also have access to other communal buildings, gardens and land belonging to the group.

A formal education programme would be devised for each individual child in consultation with their parents. At the beginning of the educational year the children would choose a personal tutor from amongst the community's education workers, and this adult would then become responsible for supervising their year's educational programme.

Let us consider how education in community might work by looking at the education of another imaginary child whom we will call Charlotte. Charlotte is nine years old, and although her reading is quite good, her writing and spelling are not. Her personal tutor immediately identifies this as an area where further work will be needed, and this is openly discussed with her in a loving and non-censorial way, so that she may understand and co-operate with the individual work her tutor will devise for her when she works on a one-to-one basis with him on two mornings each week.

Charlotte is particularly interested in horses, and opts to do a project on them this year, as well as to locate her 'community service' obligation in work with the community's animals. She will therefore spend two mornings a week working in the stables, as well as helping a little with the other animals. This work, and her project on horses, will be under the supervision of the community member responsible for the animals, who will also give her formal riding instruction on two afternoons a week.

Charlotte has also become interested in Venice, because her mother visited the city recently. She elects to do another project on this, which her personal tutor will supervise. She decides to ask for tutorial help to fully master her budding skills on the centre's computer, so that her projects can be beautifully presented. She will therefore spend another afternoon each week with one of the community's information technology experts, learning how to use both the word processing software, and an extensive DTP package. Charlotte also knows that she can go into the education centre at any time she chooses and practice her keyboard skills on the computers that are available to her there.

Apart from these commitments, Charlotte is free to organise her time as she chooses. She is likely to join a swimming class for her age group once a week, and she knows that her personal tutor is available to her at any reasonable time by arrangement, and that she will find him in the education centre three mornings a week when he will be happy to guide her work on her projects.

The educational year in community ends with the Spring Festival at the end of March, for summer is understood as a time for outdoor pursuits, for gardening and games, outings and activities. For this important annual festival children mount exhibitions of their year's work, perform plays and give concerts and demonstrations of their skills. Charlotte will ride in the display of horsemanship before an audience of local people, friends and visitors, and along with the work of all the community's other children, her finished projects may form part of the exhibition, so she has a powerful incentive to demonstrate her best skills.

Her working week is full and busy, and her skills are carefully guided and developed on an individual basis. But through her educational programme Charlotte also learns the necessity for self-organisation to meet time constraints, the art of presentation, and the value and importance of giving her time and service to the whole group of which she knows herself to be a part.

3. Present options

Whilst such ideas remain as future possibilities, for parents searching for a holistic approach to the education of their own children there is a number of practical options available in Britain at the present time.

i. Montessori Schools

Whilst Montessori herself was very much in tune with the ideas underlying a modern holistic approach to education, the degree to which the schools that carry her name fulfil her vision is very variable. Check out your local schools personally. Most cater for children only of nursery age -seven is usually the maximum age - and many are very expensive. The Association Montessori Internationale will provide lists of recognised schools.

ii. Steiner Schools

As one of the few options available for secondary education, there is an ever growing number of Steiner schools in Britain today. Deeply focused in the child's spiritual life, some are nevertheless very rigid in their application of Steiner principles which can make them feel rather fusty and old fashioned and teenagers can sometimes react badly to this. Nevertheless, this is probably the most successful and realistic option in Britain for older children if you want or need them to attend formal schools. The Steiner Fellowship will provide lists of schools in Britain.

iii. Small Schools

These are more modern in their approach, if you are fortunate enough to have a Small School in your area - lucky you! Unfortunately there are as yet very few of them, and they do not encourage families to move into the area in the hope of getting their children into the schools that exist. Better, if you have the time and energy, to set up your own, using the small school model - you will get plenty of help and advice from existing schools and from The Human Scale Education Movement which exists to promote them.

iv. Home Education

An increasingly popular option both in this country and internationally is home-based education. This is the most flexible option, and it suits some children very well, but very demanding of parents time, energy and imagination. The main disadvantage from the child's point of view can be lack of contact with other children, although this can be overcome in various ways including involvement with your local Education Otherwise group where there is one. As well as a bi-monthly newsletter, E.O. also provides a contact list of members, and organises regular summer camps and other national events for both children and adults.

Cara Martin is available to run workshops or speak to groups interested in holistic education. She is also willing to answer individual queries either by letter or by telephone.

Cara can be contacted at:

The Living Green Centre
28 Pancras Road
London NW1 2TB

Tel/Fax 0171 837 1661

Suggested reading

Bailey, A A; 1987; **Education in the New Age**; Lucis Press; London.

> Brilliant, but heavyweight, exploration of the esoteric purpose of education as the evolution of consciousness.

Carter, F; 1986; **The Education of Little Tree**; University of New Mexico Press, Albuquerque, USA.

> If you want a single book that embodies the **spirit** of holistic education, rather than its detailed methodology, this is it. Simply a delight.

Chilton Pearce; 1977; **The Magical Child**; Paladin; London.

> An interesting and valuable theory of natural child development.

Deakin, M; 1973; **The Children on the Hill**; Quartet, London.

> An extraordinary story of a dedicated mother's experiment in educational freedom for her own four children.

Freire, P; 1972; **Pedagogy of the Oppressed**; Penguin, London.

> A Marxist classic which advocates the important concept of education as a "dialogue" between "teacher" and "student".

Gatto, J T; 1992; **Dumbing us Down**; New Society Publishers; Philadelphia.

> A simply-written, crystal clear, but utterly damning, indictment of current methods of schooling written by an award-winning American teacher.

Holt, J; 1984; **How Children Fail**; Penguin; London.

> A classic analysis of the failures and inadequacies of contemporary methods of schooling.

Illich, I; 1971; **De-Schooling Society**; Harper & Row, New York.

> A brilliant analysis from a Marxist perspective of the hidden agenda of conventional schooling and its alternatives.

Liedloff, J; 1979; **The Continuum Concept**; Warner; New York.

> Drawing on her experiences whilst living with the Yequana people in the Amazon forest, Liedloff develops a fascinating theory of child-rearing within the natural evolutionary patterns of human life.

Meighan, R.; 1995; **John Holt: Personalised education and the reconstruction of schooling,** Educational Heretics Press; Nottingham.

> All ten of John Holt's books are reviewed and summarised with ample, pertinent quotations from the original texts.

Meighan, R; 1997 **The Next Learning System: and why home-schoolers are trailblazers**, Educational Heretics Press; Nottingham.

> Many families opting out of schooling are reluctant educational heretics. This book examines the research from various countries including UK and teases out the reasons why hone-schoolers are so successful - often to their own surprise and delight.

Montessori, M; 1984; **The Absorbent Mind**; Laurel; New York.

> Montessori's classic on the education of young children. Now, inevitably, somewhat dated, but still an inspiration.

Sherman, Ann; 1997; **Rules, Routines and Regimentation;**
Educational Heretics Press; Nottingham.

> Six-year-old children tell how, after one year of
> schooling, they are experiencing more of a deadening of
> the spirit than a celebration of the joy of learning.

Shute, Chris; 1993; **Compulsory Schooling Disease;** Educational
Heretics Press; Nottingham.

> An experienced teacher explores the view that. whatever
> their claims, schools are training most young people to
> be habitually subservient.

Shute, Chris; 1994; Alice Miller: **The Unkind Society,
Parenting and Schooling;** Educational Heretics Press;
Nottingham.

> The psychiatrist Alice Miller found that all the members
> of Hitler's ruling group had the same severe, authorit-
> arian upbringing and schooling. Chris Shute suggests
> that we should learn from this before history repeats
> itself.

Wissa Wassef, R; 1972; **Woven by Hand**; Hamlyn; London.

> This book documents the success of a little-
> known, but quite exceptional achievement in
> creative educational freedom, which has
> enormous significance for education as a whole.
> Sadly it is now out of print and difficult to find,
> but is worth tracking down - the British Library
> has a copy.

References

Bailey, A. A, 1987, **Education in the New Age**, Lucis Press, London.

Barrow, R, & Woods, R, 1988, **An Introduction to Philosophy of Education**, Routledge, London.

Borysenko, J, & Borysenko, M, 1994, **The Power of the Mind to Heal**, Eden Grove, Middx.

Bowlby, J, 1965, **Child Care and the Growth of Love,** Penguin, Harmondsworth, Middx.

Caddy, E, & Platts, D E, 1993, **Choosing to Love: A Practical Guide to Bringing More Love into Your Life**, Findhorn Press, Findhorn, Scotland.

Capra, F, 1983, **The Tao of Physics,** Fontana, London.

Chilton Pearce, J, 1977, **The Magical Child**, Paladin, London.

Coehlo, P, (1995), **The Alchemist**, Thorsons, London.

Deakin, M, 1973, **The Children on the Hill**, Quartet, London.

Donaldson, M, 1978, **Children's Minds,** Fontana, London.

Freire, P, 1972, **Pedagogy of the Oppressed**, Penguin, Harmondsworth, Middx.

Gatto, J T, 1992, **Dumbing us Down**, New Society Publishers, Phil., USA.

Gardner, H, 1993, **The Unschooled Mind,** Fontana Press, London.

Goleman, D, 1996, **Emotional Intelligence: Why it can matter more than IQ**, Bloomsbury, London.

Holt, J, 1984, **How Children Fail**, Penguin, London

Holt, J, 1991, **Learning all the Time**, Education Now Publishing Co-operative, Ticknall, Derbyshire.

Illich, I, 1971, **De-Schooling Society**, Harper & Row, New York.

Liedloff, J, 1979, **The Continuum Concept**, Warner Book, New York.

Miller, A, 1987, **For Your Own Good**, Virago Press, London.

Montessori, M, 1984, **The Absorbent Mind,** Laurel, New York, USA.

Mortimer, P, Sammons, P, Stoll, L, Lewis, D, & Ecob, R, 1988, **School Matters: The Junior Years** Open Books, Somerset, England.

Peck, S M, 1987, **The Road Less Travelled,** Rider, London.

Piaget, J, 1977, **The Origins of Intelligence in the Child,** Penguin, Harmondsworth, Middx.

Rose, C & Goll, L, 1992, **Accelerate Your Learning,** Accelerated Learning Systems Ltd, Aylesbury, England.

Roman, S, 1986, **Living with Joy**, H J Kramer, California, USA.

Schweinhart, L J, Barnes, H V, & Weikart, D P, 1993, **Significant Benefits: The High Scope Perry Preschool Study Through Age 27**, High Scope Press, Ypsilanti, USA.

Siegel, B S, 1988, **Love, Medicine & Miracles,** Arrow Books, London.

Szekely, E B, 1976, **The Gospel of the Essenes**, C W Daniel & Co, Saffron Walden, England.

Wissa Wassef, R, 1972, **Woven by Hand**, Hamlyn, London.

Useful Organisations

Education Now
113 Arundel Drive
Bramcote Hill
Nottingham
NG9 3FQ

Education Otherwise
PO Box 7420
London
N9 9SG
(please enclose an A5 stamped addressed envelope)

Human Scale Education Movement
96 Carlingcott
Nr Bath
Avon BA2 8AW

Montessori Society
26 Lyndhurst Gardens
London NW3 5NW
Tel 0171 435 3646

Steiner Schools Fellowship
Kidbrook Park
Forest Row
East Sussex
RH18 5JB
Tel 01342 822115